LIFE IS MORE THAN A JOB

LIFE IS MORE THAN A JOB

*A Guide for Those Who Choose Not
to Climb the Corporate Ladder*

SHEILA TILLMAN

LIFE IS MORE THAN A JOB
A Guide for Those Who Choose Not to Climb the Corporate Ladder

iUniverse books may be ordered through booksellers or by contacting:

iUniverse
1663 Liberty Drive
Bloomington, IN 47403
www.iuniverse.com
1-800-Authors (1-800-288-4677)

Because of the dynamic nature of the Internet, any web addresses or links contained in this book may have changed since publication and may no longer be valid. The views expressed in this work are solely those of the author and do not necessarily reflect the views of the publisher, and the publisher hereby disclaims any responsibility for them.

Any people depicted in stock imagery provided by Thinkstock are models, and such images are being used for illustrative purposes only. Certain stock imagery © Thinkstock.

ISBN: 978-1-5320-2255-5 (sc)
ISBN: 978-1-5320-2256-2 (e)

Library of Congress Control Number: 2017906315

Print information available on the last page.

iUniverse rev. date: 04/21/2017

CONTENTS

 INTRODUCTION

KEEPING YOUR DAY JOB

Every day thousands of employees report for work in large corporations, financial institutions, and call centers, among many others. The vast majority are not supervisors, managers, directors, or CEOs. Instead, they toil day in and day out doing the actual work that makes the corporation profitable. Some of these employees define success in terms of the money and status of management positions, and they will spend their careers climbing the corporate ladder. Scores of books have been written about how to get promoted. While it is in management's best interest to keep all workers focused on getting ahead in the company, in reality, very few employees will accomplish that goal.

This book is dedicated to employees who believe there are more important things in life than working and who define success in different ways. They have aspirations and pursuits other than their jobs and want nothing more than to work in a relatively stress-free environment and return home each day with the satisfaction of a job well done.

CHAPTER 1

A JOB IS WORK

As you walk into your job on the first day, understand this—an employer hires you to do a job, will define it, and will train you to do it. If you have trouble accepting authority or if you're one of those people who wants to "do it my way" (you know who you are), you will need to make a conscious decision to leave the attitude at the door. An employer is paying you to do the job the way he or she wants it done—and wants it done well.

Job one is to learn the job. Make no mistake—if you don't perform well, you're gone. For the first few weeks, buckle down and learn the job. Take notes, ask questions, study, practice, focus, participate, and be on time. If this sounds a lot like school, it is; if you had trouble in any of these areas as a student, now would be the time to address it. This is not the time to challenge the company's policies or procedures.

You will probably have a honeymoon period of one to two months, depending on the complexity of the job. During this period your employer will probably tolerate a few work-related mistakes, but an employer is never going to tolerate tardiness or absenteeism. You need to demonstrate that you can do the job and that you will show up to get it done. If you find that you can't grasp the fundamentals of the job in the first couple of months, you may want to look for a way to exit gracefully (an excuse could be having to care for a sick relative, an opportunity to continue your studies, or an opportunity to go on a religious mission)—anything that will look better on your work record than getting fired. Most states will allow employers to dismiss employees without explanation during the first thirty- to ninety-day probationary period.

If you are called in for a meeting and are told you are not meeting expected standards, look for a way out. Management has most likely already decided to let you go, and they will tell you that they'll be monitoring your job performance for the next week (or two) and that as long as you meet standards, everything will be okay. What this means is that everything you do on the job will be scrutinized 100 percent—you'll be in a very stressful situation. You may be able to pull it off, but consider that it will probably be difficult for even a long-term employee to survive this kind of scrutiny without making some kind of mistake.

If you have to beat a hasty retreat, don't take it personally—it probably isn't your fault. Corporations often have people training entry-level positions who have no teaching background. The trainers are selected because they do the job well, but unfortunately, the skills required to do the job do not necessarily translate to the skills required to train the job. These top performing trainers have usually not been given even a rudimentary training skills class and bring their own personal issues and baggage that can complicate their communication to a trainee. Their actual training performance is rarely monitored or evaluated. Until corporations are willing to invest in quality training, they will continue to lose potentially good employees.

Their loss. Move on.

CHAPTER 2

ATTITUDE IS EVERYTHING

A positive, confident, can-do attitude is necessary to achieve anything worthwhile in life, including in the workplace. A truly positive attitude is much more than mere acquiescence. It is a centering calm that comes from the inside out, a grounding sense of perspective, an ability to look at situations, people, and issues objectively, from a place outside of personal bias. A person with a truly positive attitude can listen and consider opposing viewpoints; can confidently express and explain both sides of an issue; can review and assess his or her personal strengths and weaknesses. People with positive attitudes don't think they can do *anything*, they're just very clear about what they can do and how to accomplish it. People who have a good attitude are centered and grounded, know who they are, and are comfortable in their own skin. They have purpose, focus, and resolve.

In the workplace, these are the employees who don't take criticism personally. They can quickly assess and pursue productive courses of action and are already planning their next steps after the proposed layoff meeting.

Unfortunately, most workplaces have usurped and twisted the concept of positiveness to mean to "do whatever we tell you and smile while you're doing it." Companies have convinced employees that absolute conformity is the only acceptable behavior. A true positive attitude comes from inside you; it is a centering calm, and the source is from outside work. You may need to make a conscious decision to act the part of the smiling, accepting employee to prevent being branded as having an "attitude problem."

The key to your own personal peace with this is to develop a core positiveness (through introspection, spirituality, and religion [see chapter 12 for discussion on religion]) that will help you understand that a role you play does not define you as a person. In other words, you are not a sellout if you choose to present a pleasant demeanor in the workplace rather an angry, sullen one. A bad attitude will be a determining factor in denying you deserved raises, interesting work assignments, and objective work assessments. If you are fortunate enough to have a coworker who exhibits a truly positive attitude, try to develop a relationship with that person and learn from him or her.

CHAPTER 3

YOU CAN'T BEAT THEM, SO JOIN THEM

In any workplace it's imperative that you develop good relationships with two groups of people: your supervisors and your coworkers. The key word here is *develop*—you will have to do some work to establish these relationships. If you decide to enter the workplace with a "what you see is what you get" attitude and do nothing, you're taking a big risk. Things may not work out okay, and these are the people you will spend eight or so hours a day with on a daily basis. It is worth putting in the necessary work to build a strong foundation with both groups.

First, your supervisor: The job of managing entry-level employees is one of the most important positions in a corporation. Supervisors manage the people who actually do the work that generates the profits. Supervisors regulate the standards and pace for the workload and the climate for the work environment, and they are in control of assessing your work. Your immediate supervisor will be a big part of making your work experience tolerable or hell.

You will know within a few days whether or not you like your supervisor; however, the real decision you will have to make is whether you are prepared to put in the effort to work with him or her. This is a critical decision that every employee needs to give deliberate, thoughtful consideration. Many employees waste their time focusing on a supervisor they feel doesn't like them, when in truth the time would be better spent deciding if they can do the job and how badly they need it. If keeping the job is important, then employees are going to have to adapt their own behavior to build a productive working relationship with the supervisor because the supervisor is not going to change. The foundation of establishing this relationship is (at a minimum) being polite, engaged, and attentive; being on time; participating with other employees; and dressing appropriately for the job.

In other words, rather than stressing over your relationship with your boss, channel your energy into doing the best job you can. If for any reason you and your supervisor get off on the wrong foot and you are unable to turn the situation around, don't stay and complain and hope things will get better, because they won't. In the corporate pecking order, a supervisor outranks an employee (and especially a new employee) *every time*. You do not have a vote in the workplace; it is not a democracy, and it is easier to change jobs than to do battle with a supervisor.

If you decide you need the job badly enough to keep working for the supervisor from hell, hunker down, keep your mouth shut, and perform your job flawlessly until you can transfer or seek other employment.

The other group central to your workplace experience are your coworkers. If you are accepted as part of this group, you will have access to lots of useful information (such as shortcuts and checklists to help you get the job done more efficiently, information on company benefits, what works and what doesn't, etc.). Coworkers can be a valuable source for non-work-related issues as well (e.g., the most affordable daycare or housing, or where to get the best deals on clothes, groceries, car repairs, etc.).

Your key to being accepted by your coworkers is to learn the job and do it well—your coworkers need to see that you are serious about the work and that you are pulling your weight.

It's imperative to be quiet and listen. The mistake a lot of new employees make is that they blab. Answer questions, but don't volunteer a lot of personal information, gossip, or political or religious views before you understand the group dynamic. Take it slow and develop relationships that you will feel comfortable with for the long-term. Make no mistake, if you don't handle these relationships carefully, your coworkers will use their own special way to deal with or even sabotage you. They will tattle—everyone makes mistakes, but they will see to it that *all* of your mistakes are brought to the attention of the supervisor. Or they will send you an e-mail detailing your error—and will copy your supervisor.

They will give others the wrong impression, suggesting you're always late, even keeping track of your lateness ("It's seven minutes after; isn't she coming in?"), or saying you "made yet another mistake."

Believe me—they won't help you. They'll tell you to check that with the supervisor when you have questions, or suggest you look up answers yourself in the policies and procedures manual.

Another institution you'll need to get comfortable with is the office grapevine, a constant source of not just gossip but of observations, trivia, and information. Sometimes the grapevine spreads malicious and untrue information, and sometimes the information is true and useful. The important thing to remember is that there will always be talk (much like the Internet). The key is to be able use the information that might be helpful to you and discard the rest.

When you work in a corporate workplace, try to be careful to share only personal information that you will feel comfortable with if it is widely disseminated (it will often end up on the grapevine), and try not to be the source of information that could be hateful for someone else. Just like the childhood game of gossip, the information will become worse and worse as it is repeated. But interestingly enough it will always be attributed to the first source—you. At some point you may become the subject of the office grapevine, and if the information is negative you can count on a coworker to bring it to your attention. It is an impossible task to find out who said what, when, and how, so don't even try. Ignore it, because someone else will be the subject in a few days.

The bottom line is this: if you can't (or don't want) to establish a decent working relationship with your coworkers, it is best to transfer to a new group or find a new job. (Your coworkers have almost as much power as your supervisor to make your work experience uncomfortable.) The longer you stay, the worse things will get, and the more damaged your work reputation will become.

CHAPTER 4

HUMAN RESOURCES IS NOT YOUR FRIEND

For some reason employees of large corporations view the human resource department as the ultimate complaint department. They believe HR is an impartial third party that will objectively evaluate their complaints and make fair decisions.

Nothing could be further from the truth. The fact is everyone who works in that department is employed by the corporation. Their salaries, bonuses, and pensions come from the corporation. The human resources department's main goals are to keep the company out of legal difficulties and to limit its liability when exposed.

If you have a personnel complaint that violates a law, HR may eventually advocate on your behalf, but only if it's to the company's benefit. This includes issues involving labor laws, such as sexual harassment, hazardous working conditions, physical threats, and the like. HR will generally jump right on these with an investigation because the corporation stands to lose big bucks if they are found in violation of the law—the caveat here is that you will need to make sure you have proof.

The mistake most employees make is that they believe HR will work on their behalf on subjective issues as well. If you believe you should have received a promotion, you deserve the job you were forced to train the new hire to do, you disagree with your most recent job rating, or you feel your coworkers just don't like you—do not go to HR, which will come down solidly in support of management.

So unless your particular situation affects the bottom line or the public perception of the company, your personal "unfair" situation is of no consequence—being fair is not a particular value of the workplace. If you feel mistreated on a personal level, first document everything concerning the issue—who, what, when, and why, record witness statements if possible or keep a list of names, make copies of all e-mails, and so on. Take a couple of days to control your anger and then consider your options (during this time, keep your job performance exemplary and your mouth shut about the issue).

As you consider your options, consider this: no matter what you've been taught or what you believe, life is not always fair. The company does not have "be fair to you" written in its mission statement. Many of us believe that right and wrong are synonymous with fair and unfair—but they are not. (Is it fair that corporations move operations from the United States to foreign countries and put thousands of Americans out of work? Or that American corporations arbitrarily decide what holidays they will honor and which they won't, thus depriving overtime to thousands of employees who are required to work on those days?)

Do not be automatically led by your coworkers. If you discuss the situation with them (and you really shouldn't), you may very well hear statements like, "I wouldn't put up with that if I were you," or "I would report that." Just remember your coworkers do not have to pay your mortgage or feed your kids. The bottom line is, you can stay on the job and forget the issue (or at least continue working as if you have); you can stay on the job and start to look for another one; or you can consult an attorney who specializes in employment issues and follow his or her advice. Once again, keep your job performance exemplary (no sniping, whining, or complaining) so you can leave with a good referral and without burning any bridges you may have to cross later if you stay with the company.

CHAPTER 5

COMPETITION

Winning, being the best, or having the most is as much a part of the corporate workplace as it is in the rest of our society. Money, power, and position are valued in a capitalistic society; the more you have, the more important you are, because those values maintain the structure of our way of life. Of course we always need people who have "less than" to fuel this way of life— you have to have more money, more power, or a more powerful position than someone else, or what's the point? In corporate-speak you must have a higher title or pay grade to have more power, be worth more, and provide those "below you" something to aspire and work toward. It's like a giant Ponzi scheme based on the continued contributions of those who want more and more.

The capitalism model is alive and well in the corporate workplace—the higher the position, the larger the salary, and the more decision-making power you have. Competition is at the center of the capitalistic pyramid; there will always be winners and losers. Management often tries to capitalize on this by pitting worker against worker, group against group for job ratings, raises, and recognition. They will say that healthy competition is good, when in reality it's not good in the workplace. Competition means winners and losers, and productivity suffers when a portion of the workforce feel like losers. Working to be better than someone else only causes bad feelings, distrust, and in some cases cheating.

The better plan would be to set a realistic goal and let coworkers compete to meet or exceed that goal, rather than against one another. If the employee does not meet the goal, he or she will focus on his or her own performance to find ways to improve.

There seems to be an attitude in corporations that there should be 10 percent of employees on top and 10 percent on the bottom. This is based on goals that change sometimes quarterly to make sure that this is the result. If they get too many employees in the top range and too few on the bottom, managers will say the goals were set incorrectly. If the initial goal is realistically based on what will make the corporation profitable, for instance if the goal is 90 percent completed sales or 85 percent customer satisfaction, and the company overall makes that goal, then all employees who contributed to that goal should be compensated. Corporations usually buy into the idea that the only way to achieve better results is to pit worker against worker.

Managers and supervisors have a tendency to use the stick-and-carrot approach—they assume workers have no personal ownership or pride in their performance and have to be browbeat and cajoled to perform well. There are few (if any) employees who get up in the morning and think, *I'm going to work today and do the worst possible job I can.*

The bottom line is that you will continually be subjected to competition in the corporate workplace. The trick is to not get caught up in the hype surrounding it and to not lose sight of your personal self-worth. There will be times when you see coworkers receive performance reviews or bonuses that you believe they didn't deserve. Understand that as long as you are in a competitive environment these things are going to happen (look at the doping scandals in sports or the voting scandals in politics).

It may be a hard truth to own, but if you're not willing to cheat—and you understand that true success is not defined by a salary, a title, or a performance rating—then your option is to come to work every day and do the best possible job you can. Eventually, people (and corporations) who cheat always get caught.

CHAPTER 6

WHISTLEBLOWERS

Job one for all large corporations is to maximize profits. Corporations employ an army of senior managers, attorneys, statisticians, project managers, and others to establish and vet business practices that will enhance their profitability. As a result, corporations are heavily invested in their policies and practices, and their procedures quickly become embedded in the workplace culture. So when employees who have not been part of the decision-making process challenge the morality or legality of their methods, corporations usually don't respond well.

When technicians at Volkswagen alerted their supervisors that software installed in their diesel vehicles was illegal, they were ignored. When VA hospital employees voiced their concerns about the level of care being provided, they were ignored. When bank employees tried to sound the alarm on unreliable credit practices prior to the unprecedented bank failures of the early 2000s, and more recently in 2016, when Wells Fargo employees tried to sound the alarm on hundreds of accounts that were being opened illegally, they were ignored. No changes were made to any of these issues until they were exposed by parties outside of the corporations—press, regulatory agencies, and watchdog groups.

If you are required to do something in the course of your job that you believe is illegal or wrong (not something you just don't like but something that is actually wrong), send an e-mail to your supervisor or manager that clearly details the issue and the impact (keep a copy). You will probably get a reply that says, "We will look into this" (translation: mind your own business), or "all of our policies have been approved by legal" (translation: mind your own business). Or you may get no reply at all (further translation: mind your own business).

Understand that corporations usually operate and profit from a strategy of doing something until you get caught. Corporations implement policies in a way that will be most profitable. If those policies are proven later to be wrong, the corporation can say (in effect), "Sorry, we'll change that right away"—meanwhile keeping the millions of dollars that they collected while the questionable or illegal policy was in place. Even if the corporation pays a fine, the thousands of people who were victimized by the policy in the first place are never compensated. Corporations change their policies under pressure from regulators, politicians, or large groups of customers; they are certainly not going to change for someone they pay.

As an employee who believes that something wrong is going on and whose alert has been ignored, you now have a decision to make—fight or fold. If you decide to fight, know that it is going to be a long, stressful uphill battle. You will need to bring attention to the issue via media and possibly regulatory and law enforcement agencies. You will be vilified by managers and coworkers, and the probability is high that you will be fired. Depending on the issue, you may even be sued by the corporation. Being a whistleblower requires that you prepare yourself mentally and financially.

If you decide to fold (and not take on Goliath), do two things for yourself: first, *let it go.* Don't continue to beat a dead horse, and don't beat up on yourself. You have done everything you can, so be comforted by the fact that corporate wrongdoing is almost always exposed at some point and when it is, you will at least have the satisfaction that you tried to raise the alarm.

Second, try to harness the level of righteous indignation and energy you feel about this issue and channel it to some other important issue outside of the workplace—homelessness, teen pregnancy, literacy, hunger, community outreach, and so forth. There are countless projects you can work on that will make a difference and give you personal satisfaction.

CHAPTER 7

RULES ARE RULES

If you work in the corporate world, you will often hear the phrase "Sorry, but those are the rules; there's nothing I can do." Rules are important. They provide the structure for our society. Rules help us determine acceptable personal behavior and what to expect from others. There are rules for every facet of our lives—school, sports, clubs, driving, church, and the like. We are conditioned to accept and obey the rules and know there are consequences if we don't. We don't like people who don't play by the rules.

It is important to your job satisfaction that you understand that corporations will occasionally break or bend the rules. Money and/or power trump them every time. If you stay with a corporation long enough, you will eventually see evidence of this.

For example, attendance rules may state that only four unapproved absences are allowed, but you will have coworkers who have had more but faced no consequences. The job bulletin may state that certain requirements are mandatory for a particular position, but you will observe employees who meet none or few of the requirements selected for the job.

We want to believe that everyone follows the rules, but they don't—not in life and certainly not in the workplace. It is fruitless for you to try to battle these situations. You will only bang your head against the corporate wall, and the only result will be the bruises on your head. About the only thing you can do is to note these incidents in your work diary, in case it becomes necessary at some point to show that there is a history of breaking the rules in this particular environment.

CHAPTER 8

CHANGE FOR CHANGE'S SAKE

One of the mantras of corporate life is that the only constant is change.

Corporations are constantly changing things in the workplace—policies, practices, personnel, location, job duties, hours of operation, and so forth. They justify these actions by saying they make the company more efficient, increase profits, and/or address customer concerns.

The problem is that corporations rarely assess the long-term personnel or technological impacts of the changes and implement them without proper training or regard for the impacts of the end-to-end processes they are changing. If a corporation believes there is a chance to increase the bottom line, they will crack the whip of change without concern for how far the tip travels.

Frontline employees (who are typically not consulted or considered) sometimes make the mistake of thinking their opinion about changes to their work activities matter—it doesn't.

Comments such as, "This isn't going to work," "Customers won't like this," or "This is going to cause more work" are not productive. Employees are better served by focusing on learning as much as they can about how they are expected to implement changes. This may be a bitter pill to swallow, but resolve to comply with the change exactly as it is presented. Don't try to improve the process or make it run more smoothly; do exactly as you're told. If the change is as ill-conceived as you think it is, it will fail, and things will return to the status quo, or management will be forced to rework the change and hopefully consult with the people who actually do the work to help make the change work.

Another stressor in a constantly changing work environment is the persistent underlying threat of employee reduction due to cost saving measures. It is a curious fact that corporations adopt changes based on their cost savings but rarely actually track the savings. Corporations usually choose to equate the success of the change implementation rather that any actual savings. This may be because a lot of these changes end up costing the corporation more than they save.

In order to keep your personal stress level down, try to ignore downsizing rumors. This is one time that you need to find the strength to deal with a situation that you have no control over. Still, it never hurts to polish your résumé and perhaps send out a few copies to test the waters. Working around downsizing rumors is one thing, but don't be caught with your pants down either.

CHAPTER 9

WHAT TO WEAR

The first thing you may want to do when deciding on your corporate wardrobe is to give some thought as to what you want to achieve. Do you want to show off your assets? Do you want to attract the attention of the opposite sex? Do you want to show off your superior fashion sense? Do you want to make a statement that you will dress any way you choose?

No problem, as long as you're clear on how you may be perceived in the workplace. Go for it. Just be prepared for the consequences—gossip, disapproving looks, snide remarks. If on the other hand you want to keep your work hours as stress free and drama free as possible, you may want to consider leaving the "look at me" clothing for after hours and the weekend.

Consider these two techniques. First, look at yourself in a full-length mirror once you are dressed and make any necessary adjustments. Second, use the uniform principle: build a wardrobe of a few color-coordinated outfits that suit your style, and rotate wearing them. You will save a ton of money and will always look presentable.

CHAPTER 10

FOOD

It is surprising, but food plays several interesting roles in corporate life. Management will occasionally provide low-cost goodies for the worker bees—pizza, doughnuts, bagels. These treats are usually provided for group results that will be worth big bonuses for management and big profits for the company. Go ahead and enjoy the food because these are the only fruits of your labor you will ever likely see. Always keep in mind that eating a few snacks is not a substitute for reasonable wages, health care benefits, and time off.

There are several office "food commandments" in the workplace that you need to be aware of.

First, thou shall participate in office potlucks. Bring something that is professionally prepared (from a bakery, delicatessen, grocery store, etc.). Don't bring beverages, napkins, paper plates, and utensils unless you are specifically asked to—you will be labeled as cheap if you never bring actual food. Above all, never eat anything from the potluck if you haven't brought something.

Second, thou shall be careful of which homemade potluck goodies you eat. As you go through the line, think about which coworkers have pets, which might have their adorable children help them in the kitchen, and which ones don't wash their hands after using the restroom. If you're pressured to take items you aren't comfortable eating, take a small amount and throw it away later.

Third, thou shall not steal food. There isn't a corporate workplace refrigerator anywhere that hasn't been hit by a thief at some time. When this does happen you will find your coworkers buzzing—there will be those who want cameras installed, or those who want to set traps (like making brownies with laxatives), and there will be those who spend an inordinate amount of time trying to figure out who the culprit is. But remember—if you have a coworker who is willing to risk stealing a lunch, that person may just be hungry and can't afford to buy food (we've all been there). Don't assume that because you're doing okay everyone else is—try a little charity.

Fourth, as you are beginning your work career, if you can discipline yourself to bring food from home (rather than buy food every day), you will save a ton of money.

Get creative. Lunch doesn't have to be always a sandwich and chips. Think deviled eggs, salads, casseroles, or leftovers. And try to work in some type of exercise on your lunch hour. Even if it is only fifteen to twenty minutes of walking, you will benefit in the long term.

CHAPTER 11

FOR BLACK EMPLOYEES ONLY

Black Americans face discrimination in almost every facet of their lives. The 2016 Urban League 'State of Black America' report shows that Black rates of unemployment have consistently remained about twice that of white rates across time regardless of education. Of those Blacks hired, they are fired, downsized or phased out of their positions at a disproportionate rate compared to their white counterparts. CNN's documentary 'Black in America' reported on the policing tactics used by police departments around the country to specifically target young Black men. The Pew Research Center has released studies that show Black Americans experience subtle and overt discrimination from preschool all the way through college. The 'Atlantic Daily' published an article titled 'Being Black – but not too Black in the workplace'. The article focuses on the behaviors necessarily employed by Black professionals to blend in to their work environments. Very little has been written about how Black Americans can cope with the day to day stereotypical-actions taken against them in the workplace.

The first hurdle black employees have to clear is to accept that everyone is not always treated equally and that because of preconceived notions, many of your coworkers are waiting to see you fail. If you buy into the fantasy that everyone is equal and is pulling for you to succeed, you will probably spend most of your time feeling resentful when you figure out that is not the case.

The truth is individual employees are not treated equally in any corporate workplace, anywhere, anytime. You will not be given any measure of confidence in your abilities or the benefit of the doubt for your mistakes. You will be presumed guilty of all the negative stereotypes until your job performance proves you capable. So what can you do? Learn the job better than anyone else—aim to be the go-to person. There is nothing more prized in the workplace than a job well done.

Until you have reached that pinnacle, be aware that the stereotypes are always out there, stalking you. For example, if you're late, it will be attributed to your inability to be on time. So always arrive early. If you make mistakes on the job, they will be attributed to your inability to learn. So learn the job better than anyone else. If you laugh easily and often, you will be labeled as boisterous or loud or unprofessional. So tone it down a notch while you are at work. If you are quiet, you will be labeled as unfriendly or unsociable, so you will need to make an effort to be at a minimum pleasant to everyone in the workplace (in other words, you will need to be nice to people you don't like).

You will also need to give careful consideration to three

attitudes and the associated behaviors that are prevalent in the black community: "telling it like it is," recognizing perceived disrespect and the resulting retaliation, and "what you see is what you get." None of these unmodified attitudes will serve you well in a corporate workplace.

"Telling it like it is," speaking your mind, or speaking the truth is rarely an asset in the workplace. First, no one cares. Second and more importantly, you will be labeled a big mouth and not a team player. You will scare off prospective mentors and will become the go-to person for all of your coworkers who will want you to raise all the issues that they don't have the courage to raise on their own.

Recognizing and retaliating against perceived disrespect in the workplace will keep you very busy and will earn you a reputation as difficult to work with. Considering that you will be working with many people from different backgrounds and different cultures and different beliefs, it is almost a given that at least one of your coworkers is going to say or do something, sometime that you may consider offensive. If you value personal peace, it will be better for you to assume that your coworkers have no malicious intent. (Most times they really don't.) The minute you start responding to every perceived slight in a combative way, you will come across as a complainer. Sure, some slights will be deliberate, but the best revenge in the workplace is to maintain a high job performance and ignore them. If you want to fight disrespect, join one of the many established antidiscrimination groups that are striving to make a real difference.

"What you see is what you get": this attitude projects behaviors that suggest you're not open to change or to learning new things. This attitude scares off those coworkers who may be different from you and shuts down meaningful communication. As a result, you will miss out on insights, support, and information that could be valuable to you.

The bottom line is this—before you accept a job in a corporate workplace, understand that corporations will expect you to perform in lockstep without rocking the boat. Why is this an issue for you? Black people have a shared history of creating stellar achievements by not conforming (in music, fashion, dance, social issues, etc.). To be clear, you cannot suppress who you are, nor should you. In fact, you should honor, respect, and cherish your heritage—a lot of people paid a big price so you could be employed at all. Make an informed choice. If you feel that homogenizing your behavior to fit in is not something you can (or want) to do, remember that there are jobs in other fields that require the same hard work, effort, and focus but will welcome your enthusiasm, creativity, and passion.

CHAPTER 12

FOR CHRISTIANS IN THE WORKPLACE

If you are a Christian, there are some things that that you need to think about before you begin working in a corporate workplace.

First, if national surveys are to be believed, more than half of your coworkers won't even know what a Christian is. (The Pew Research Center reports declining levels of religious belief and practice among the generation of Americans born in the last two decades.) Second, anything you *say* will probably not convince any of them to convert to Christianity. And third, when you identify as a Christian, your behavior at work will be closely scrutinized; you will be baited and probably personally attacked.

A Christian by definition is someone who believes that Jesus died and shed his blood to atone for our sins and that he rose from death after three days to ascend to heaven, assume all power, and sit at the right hand of God. That belief does not make Christians perfect. In fact, a Christian's journey is a continuous personal examination of his or her own faults and continuous work toward personal improvement. Christians commit their lives to trying to develop strong personal relationships with Christ and to live as dictated by the precepts outlined in the Bible. This involves a lifetime of hard work, struggles, and setbacks.

Unfortunately, many of your coworkers think a Christian is a Goody Two-shoes who never has any fun and doesn't want anyone else to have fun either. Which brings us to the second point—you will never convince any of your coworkers that what they believe isn't true by anything you *say*. It's like trying to convince them that a cake tastes sweet when they don't know what a cake is.

Since most workplaces don't allow (or they frown upon) any discussion of religion, you may want to consider sharing your faith another way—by showing it. If you believe what the Bible says, your internal work toward becoming a better person should cause some external changes in your behavior.

So as you progress on your Christian journey, your patience, kindness, charity, peace, and love should become more and more evident to your coworkers. This will give you an opportunity to answer their questions about why you react differently in a meaningful way.

Lastly, if you insist on making statements like "I don't do that; I'm a Christian" or "My faith doesn't allow that," be prepared for backlash. It will be like waving a red flag. Everything you do will be observed closely, and you will hear statements like "How can she or he call herself or himself a Christian and do that?" or "We all know what the Christian is going to say"—or, worse yet, you will be excluded from some gatherings, meetings, or work assignments based on some mistaken perceptions held by your coworkers.

Christians should not despair – they have internal resources that make them uniquely suited for success in any workplace. Christians have access to a peace that is 'beyond all understanding'; to a helpmate (the Holy Spirit) who will lead and guide them in all that is true and good; and to a source who holds all power and glory. And Christians come with a built in warning – 'all weapons formed against them will not prosper'.